also by Neeli Cherkovski

Poetry:

Fronteras Rotas 2005
Leaning Against Time 2004
Elegy for Bob Kaufman 1996
Animal 1996
Ways in the Wood 1993
Clear Wind 1984
Love Proof 1983
Public Notice 1976
The Waters Reborn 1975
Don't Make a Move 1973

Biographies:

Bukowski: A Life (revised edition) 1997
Hank: the Life of Charles Bukowski 1991
Ferlinghetti: A Biography 1979

Essays:

Whitman's Wild Children (revised edition) 1999
Whitman's Wild Children 1988

from the
Canyon
Outward

poems by **Neeli Cherkovski**

R. L. Crow Publications 2009

From The Canyon Outward

Acknowledgements –
Various forms of some of these poems
have previously appeared in:
*OnTheBus, Poesy, 9th Street
Laboratories* (http://9thstlab.blogspot.com),
Beatitude and *Generación*

The poems: *The Knowing Without Name,
Conspiracy, Chapultepec Park, Guadalupe,
Mis Manos, and Windows*
appeared in *Fronteras Rotas*:
Mexico City, Mexico, 2005

Conspiracy and *Windows* appeared in the
Hungarian journal *Puskin Utca*

Front cover photo (Vallejo St., North Beach, S.F.) by Bill Gainer
Back cover photo by Dennis Letbetter
Cover design by R. L. Crow Publications.

R. L. Crow Publications
P.O. Box 262, Penn Valley, CA 95946
info@rlcrow.com
www.RLCrow.com

ISBN: 978-0-9722958-1-9
Library of Congress Control Number: 2009928575

for John Landry

Contents –

from the
Canyon
Outward

Lost in the Canyon

lost in the canyon far from home
here the ferns drip
elk brush against the lower cliff

stop and listen to footsteps
of a fallen god, smile
when he reaches for your groin
from which justice measures the meaning
we offer to the land
where we are condemned to abide

his lips touch my cheeks
I turn in the tide, pushed by sea breaks
I descend the salt steps to his chamber
of anemones and oval gray agate

his woman is a leopard on my tongue
if I do not speak, he may vanish
with the emerging light
I held his body
in my garden of lilac
I crept along ridges
below the constellations

he taps my shoulder when the water rises
we walk up the cliff and touch sails
half-buried in fog

the decades are reborn
in the mine of memory, I know
whenever I travel it is for the log I keep
in this cabin where
lanterns burn across the night

Quake

again, heading over
the pass, my father
shifts to the right and
the rock jerks enough
so that the dog
grows nervous,
he growls, the
owl peeks into
daylight, a waitress
at the Summit Cafe
spills coffee
in a highway
patrolman's
lap, the Etruscan
idol falls to the concrete
floor, a flood of
phone calls
jam the line,
we drive down
further to the
dry, hot center
of conceit,
we derive
pleasure in the
deepening cry
of the sun
as the land
settles, we pass the
old depot and drive over
a rocky hillside
into the heart of the
quake, it is
so alive
in our minds, we
cherish the
tremor

In the Northern Cascades

just to turn and bend
the snow around those rocks
that jut from the body
of the mountain
or to turn away
and run my eyes across your eyes
to the peaks
of other places

to be mindful of the ice caves
and to not cross the chain link boundary
or we might slip away
forever, the muse
is awake, I see the memory
of dawn and
the snow plows
on the high terrain

I rub my hands
together, crystals fall
out of my flesh,
red tailed hawks
fly above the horizon
you turn
and maybe you feel
the storm
as I feel it, how it has come
and gone, it will come
once more

just to know
the motion and to be here
in the garden
of ice, to reach for a rock
with black markings, to turn
the rock into a feather
and let it float
into the arms of air,

to believe in wisdom
and in the snowflake, to say
the world is a drunk
walking toothless
in the afternoon

we are about to return
to the lodge, I am compelled
to lean on the sun
as it wanders, to resist
leaving my homage
to the foolish monk
who froze
on another
mountain
where the dragons
were fierce and
wily, they could wait
for the summer fires
to rise from the low meadow

a light snow
falls, we have to
leave, the chair lift lurches
into the swift
metallic stream, more
snow, a deer below
with tall antlers, we know
where we are going
because we have been there
before, the plows glow, I hear
the engines
of the sky and the roar
of the rising wind

I turn around, a dangerous
thing to do, any day now

our ride will end anytime
now and the vanquished
will dance in a field of newly
fallen snow, this is the one sure thing
in a time of uncertainty, pay
attention to the change, listen
to the chains and the pulleys, reach
for the snow
with your gloved palm
and grasp it

West of Mentone

I forgive memory, and hide
in the after-glow, step onto a full moon
where trees go down, they are
piled for removal by great
yellow trucks arriving in
the afternoon, the drivers have
faces of jade, their engines remain
on idle in this land
of ceremony and brittle leaves

west of Mentone vineyards
held before the hills
and adjacent mountains, the climbing
roots and branches shed one color
and took another, depending, the
shades of being were cast
like a net, a man had a monkey
in a cage, further west
Virginia Dare vineyards and
the last orange groves

we brought the vines and
we take them away, they exist
far back in time and leap to
the present over the hills and
dried summer grass

we learn to leap and in falling
flail our arms, we know how wrong
we were and now we are okay, we
talk straight and sort things out
when the structures fail, we wonder
who threw what away, who abandoned
what, why are we struggling?

what light lights your way? snow falls
on Mount San Gorgonio, above the ruins
eons scramble, war seems insane
in that ancient epic, vineyards

mourn for a righteous hand, the
morning is solitary, down go
the groves, the vineyards vanish

it's tiresome thinking of ways
not to hear drums and bugles
anymore, to lie before the canopy
and listen to the sublime nothing
as it falls, I am trying to remain

I hope to sit in the garden
under the avocado tree and read
Mindfulness by Martin Heidegger
not straight through but enough
and to lean back in my chair

we were in the land, woven to it
lost in the mud as winds shift
knowledgeable in how shadows
follow a path to steep ravines
against the mountains

west of Mentone, north of the groves
the first enticement of alpine air, a
slippery slope, deer and black
bear, to the east the mountains
rise higher, snow divides, everywhere
we need to be seen, even
alone, burdened in disbelief

further west the Spanish mission's
thick adobe walls, high windows
and strong beams, a path
leads to a wire fence, then
asphalt and concrete, to the east
past Mentone and across the high passes
a sense of what meaning
is attached to meaning, we
follow the deities to their demise

Lorca in the Morning

early in the morning
Federico Garcia Lorca
walks along the Bixby Canyon path
to Ferlinghetti's camp
with a gypsy guitar
and a box of moonlight he has stored

I offer the last coffee in the pot,
he accepts graciously,
we sit before the soon to deepen sun
and watch old logs burn down

I turn over a log to expose
the red hot skin,
it burns the soul
just looking at it,
there are whorls of slash and burn,
ashen masks, trails of woe,
bunches of bad thinking
and lost opportunity clinging to the inferno
I've exposed

I throw dirt on the fire
when we decide to leave, the tin coffee cups
go into a soapy bowl
by the cabin door

Lorca walks at my side,
his guitar is now a horse prancing
up and down the shore,
we watch for seals,
two appear out of the roof of a wave...

go back to your ocean room
I command,
go back and bring me an albatross,
bring me Treasure Island,
bring me a deeper song

than the one sung by the somber sea
a deeper song says Federico
send me to the blue,
dapple my eyes with salt and memory,
let me stay until noon,
don't send me back just yet,
I'll read my Whitman Ode
and the King of Harlem poem

go back to your grief, Federico,
return to your country filled
with crushed desire,
the flies are swarming
over a mass grave,
the lice are feasting behind
an iron gate,
go back to sleep, leave me alone,
great poet of Spain

back at camp
a new fire glows,
I warm beans and fry a pork chop
in deep fat,
the windmill creaks,
a single hummingbird
darts into view and finds his palace
on the air
in a clearing

Mis Manos

I turn a doorknob in the hallway
of the poor hotel, the demon in my bed
has one hundred thousand fingers
and he calls for me to lie down
beside him

only for a few minutes friend
because the sky is the color of
my father who slices air
with a gold machete

when I'm outside again
the street is a mud puddle
curandero
stands under the same tree
with malevolent indifference

my hands are
made of clay

the sky
made in cloudland
by men who speak
a language of green factories
hammered into place
by people who
disappear and reappear
turn visible, invisible

my hands are filled
with the mud of a village
in the highlands of
Chiapas, Indians
are light, noble, quick
to turn their eyes
from mine

my hands are horrible
they are of
wood and dank shadows

and many times each day
I descend into the streets
to find myself imitating
four hundred or more
sets of hands attached
to an imaginary beast

it's a passing dream
and I let it fall
as rain falls
in San Cristobal de las Casas
far back in my history

I turn and the indigenas turn
earth grabs me
the sky trembles as tribes move
inside me, I think of the next bus
south to Talisman or north
to an eagle with dusty eyes
and handsome fangs

mariachis move from bar to bar
prostitutes follow, the sallow
gang from Mexico City
keeps fucking around
with two blondes from Switzerland
who strut through the plaza

all good things and more
and less and more
or less and many things
to do, to see, to fear
to forget

Windows

I will build
a forest in the grass
of Washington Square
where we wandered arm in arm
worrying about splendor
and what it means
to share a bed

forgive branches
growing from my dreams
as I curve my body
toward the confusion
of anguish
falling out of you

windows call to doors
in the hollow of a mother's anger
in the dreadnought of vision
and slam shut
when you turn from me
facing that which I fear

smooth slender hips
of woman I will never be

Man of Twilight

the needle in my lover's mouth
pigeons on his breast
trees growing from his dreams
windows sprouting on his stomach
all the natural world
full-blown and abundant
he speaks love with silence
fashions me from clay
takes my eyes to make diamonds
he stores in his brain

someday he will piece the world
out of me and throw wind
on dark dust and even
familiarize my heart with leaves
being far from the unspeakable

man of twilight

A Fencing Master

on the air,
dancer, fencing master,
designer of patterns based
on the stellar regions, the warrior avoids
my morning fire

one coal cracks, the other follows, the wasp
is a formidable foe, there is a nest
high up in an eave of the cabin,
we come to sort the limits,
to limber our unlovely lumber
past the dunes

the coals invade, they invite,
long lover lost
with a wasp sting,
bitter taste, go voyager down
the doom of insect eyes,
we cannot support
anarchy, we cannot live
without a center
that sustains

Conspiracy

I'm eating the furniture, friends arrived, amazed,
they don't know what to say, preferring to sit
on remaining chairs, whispering, "what's wrong?
he's been depressed, but this we didn't expect!"
they thought I'd lie down on the central valley floor
kissed with rhubarb, cotton, seedless grapes,
bathing in asteroid light

I'm alone, fearful of never finding
armadas that once crawled on my skin

the credit furniture department doesn't offer
antique love, or dispensations on loss
of the bison, but I am bisoning the afternoon

walking along the shore of a famous bay, preoccupied
with loss of love, needing to know how soon
I'd become completely a thing of wood

I'd wish no sutras on my friends,
nor easy enlightenment, simply
to wade in a secret cove, find abalone, starfish and anemone
breathing early California

I digest dining room tables
and television sets,
stoves and microwave ovens
are not exempt. yesterday I ate several telephones
and heard lonesome operators, wailing

today I'm busy devouring the back door
wanting to know
who I'll be in the vast conspiracy

Bukowski Makes the Huntington Library

Hank, you were right
to hold the city between your teeth
and shake it
I know that now, learning
on the drive down last month
to speak at the library
where they house your archive
I had things to say about the ease
of your being, I guess
the curator knew the worst I could say
is that the land swelled within
your grasp, the sea
of protest calmed within
a wide understanding that deepens
the divide between us,
your land of sexy blondes and
tough men with rotten teeth
watering their lawns, your landlady
blues, your leaking sink, Hemingway
in the bathtub,
I saw the hills divide into
sections, thigh and breast, leg
and neck, torso and shoulder,
the highway spun our sorrow

would we find the museum
on time? do they want me to read a poem
in your honor? answer questions?
we inched uphill past the century plants and
dry mesquite knowing that the land would flatten
into the great, grave-minded basin

you and I drank the sober drafts
of sultry summer back in 68' and 69'
while our soldiers fielded Vietnam
we'd storm through
the beatitudes, I wanted your
self-assurance, your grip, time
pulled me into the roaring asphalt

and dragged you to the heights
this is today and today feels like nowhere
except everything, I see Linda, your
love, we embrace, we walk
together through long halls, "here
are the smoking ruins of
Jack London and this
is the Ellesmere Chaucer," imagine,
down a narrow passage to a door
with a security timer, and into a room
where the manuscripts of Charles Bukowski
await the curator's hand
theft is an issue at the Huntington Library,
even scholars have larceny
secreted in their nimble fingers, touching
a Coleridge notebook, leafing through
a Shakespeare folio, now leaping
onto the backside of Bukowski
yeah, Hank, I love you, I hate, I love, I
climb the stairs with a microphone in my lapel
so the answers I give will rise like condors
over the far distant mountains that somberly
push my old city into its shadowy grave
I tell them to think of palm trees
and unending boulevards, to regard
the end as a beginning,
to forgive themselves
for the empty pages of their own design
you might have been proud
of what I said and
how I spoke with such authority
in the grim business
driving home was
largely uneventful, they
sent a letter of thanks
and invited me to soar
over the Basin one last time
with/without you,
alive and alone

Love at Night

to recognize the power love protects,
to snap a picture of the night,
a body in the shade of a soul next to your own,
to see the form, to be in the fire, the blue
on top of a blue flame,
crossing the rough alluvial,
a mind like your own torn in the name of love
close down the light, find your conspirators
in the shadow by your bed, the watch
is luminous when you press a button, it tells you
how little we understand, it instructs you
toward the foliage where grammar decomposes,
you feel the salt, you touch the glare, you fear
failure, you awaken, alone, a realist, as the big hand
meets the abyss and lingers
your love consumes a torn page,
single letters flee from
the dancing word,
your love turns into the form,
pages flap, blood
surges, roses glow
under a white mantle
see how it feels
to look on rings of sight, sad corridor
into deeper night
just to seize his arm as he sleeps, place
your arm against his, find
how others feel, what do they say when the rapture wanes
deep in night? how do they name
rummaging silence?
just to be
in the thrust,
to weave in and out of darkness, to express
in unwritten language
what we know of desire towering,
how to break ideas down,
when to step over boundaries,
in what manner to close the book,
how to bring time down around his sleeping

torso, to never touch while touching, to never speak
as the torrent continues, to put an end
to fear, to say this fear
will no longer overwhelm, to see these animals
who are there in the center of a knowing without name,
to push these wild birds against the body
of the person you love,
all this time you have spoken
in a language hewn from the forms, to think back to them,
the shape of a door, a window, to reform
a voice, to redefine
the roses, to bend
the trees, to think of how those trees
stood in one long line, how the birds
flew from branch
to branch and you tipped your finger
against the silence
of your love, you said
the word so many times, what is
this night? why does it
turn into a crane
made of blue paper
and sit on the shelf by the books?
why the treacherous greeting
and the trembling arm? where
do the wild birds go? when does
the torrent cease
destroying the books?
why does doubt stretch
over his forehead? does he awaken
somewhere else? is this merely
a form of love, but not a river or a
surge of rocks scattered
on a strong shoulder of the mountain?
come and whisper
as the night crawls, come
to the precipice, who follows
the phantom animals? which one of us
reads the footprint

of the beast? why do these forms
turn into deer in a deep
and tremulous moment like
the other night, not like this one
of sustaining rain?
you touch when you are not touching, you hear
his name as the years snag on the branches
of the trees, you open
the windows as limber fingers reach,
who will go to the ruins
and find him there? the shade
is a diamond, the shadow
is a voice from the fleeing birds, it takes
only one route to get to the
surge, he waits as the torrent
grows in intensity, you hear
what he knows of the plants, you feel
how he breathes, you hold
his breathing, you make
a circle and find a way
to be there when the sky talks of dying,
you think maybe there is no such thing
as an end, you make
a path to the ruins, you send
the man to find a way
back to the animals, you fight
for them, you struggle to live with them
you wish we could soar and not have to question
the shape of the night

The Word Strikes

the word strikes at the core
yet who will know the damage done
in these corridors
where sand meets the glittering emptiness
of your open palm?

go take the irony
and feed it, give to your friend
what this strangeness offers,
we feed ourselves on the ambrosia, we toss
our loathing and plead

so strange to see you
turn into a wave, so clear are the currents
rising, may we abide
as the unreachable spreads, go find
the single gull in flight

so, you endure, but only as a mountain,
you have cut from the dry planet
and made men talk, I cut my vision
in half, I see the cypress clinging to the word

A Deeper Snow

there it remains, not a happy thing, joyless
in fact, the crumbling ruins of her fingers, a restless
mind, how do they say it? the mind is fevered,
while up on the high passes none of this matters,
the mind is lost in meaningless argument,
high mountain grass rushes
to the mouth of the sun,
a quiet kingdom beneath the rocks erupts,
the poet does not understand
more than she can grasp with her fingers,
her father falls off the moon, drenched
in failure, a phantom mother devours
the shadow creviced against granite,
high in the air the unconscious mind struggles
to bend by the brush, stones speak out of turn
as a distant swath of snow ripens
against a phalanx of pine

a deeper snow will settle in, mourning will begin
(again), the mind, though gone, will
be remembered, taken in hand, how lonely, how
unloved, what moves the mountain to be there
in the afternoon? a trail of leaves
leads to false places, the meadow
is a garage, the voices are discordant,
above it all, emptiness, inside of it all, emptiness,
in the empty eye a strand of information, ripples,
defects, animosities, drums, flutes,
on the top of it, deeper snow, it hardens
when a tough wind learns the curve of the fingers,
the poet remains,
she remembers,
she will fashion a means

Chapultepec Park

in Chapultepec
a wiry father
lifted his sons
high in the air
so high I thought maybe
they'd never come down
but they came
as rain, deep with song and rumors
of time's end, they held fire
and dust in their tiny hands,
I saw Mexico pass, a serpent
a deep translucent pond
and a wild crush
of bodies,
the fiery movement
of people from place to place,
enormous clouds
fell from one boy's hand,
the other child held
a white rabbit that leapt
onto a playground
and hopped
in all directions at once,
the father bought snow cones
and popcorn, his wife
watched her sons as they became
cormorants, she laughed
when they were snakes, she smiled
when they were jaguars, she whistled
when they ran
through grass and climbed trees and came down
jumping, the father
threw them into the air,
they were a sensation
in the crowded park, people
came from suburbs and from towns
not yet swallowed
by the grasshopper,

the boys performed
as true artists should, frenzied and
miraculously connected to the fever
of faces and hands, to the fear and
dark musing
of those in attendance,
an honor guard of soldiers marched
from the castle on the hill
hardly out of boyhood themselves,
from villages
of corn and cattle, dark faces, dark eyes,
they came to clap and laugh, to whisper
in the ears of young women, to show-off
their bright military clothing and to watch
the two children fly above the city,
on that day every flight but theirs
was suspended, two brown
bodies in the blue,
one held a snow cone, the other
a bag of popcorn, both were giving names
to impossible feats,
it was another carnival,
a day for celebration, one more
feast in a country
of plazas and fountains, of fortune and
brass bands, the father
called on his sons to strive harder,
they sent vast herds
of cattle into the park and plenty of roasted
corn and snow from the volcano,
the father sat on a green bench,
his sons beside him, his
wife with a baby in her arms,
the baby with a butterfly on his fingertip,
the crowds with every pueblo
written on their faces, pre-ordained, every
field and all roads,
one boy threw down a cat, another

raised his own small arms
and made the city a teeming heart,
one massive breath,
it was time to go home,
people left,
gates were shut and locked,
the sky became populated
with deep resentments
of lonely men and women,
the streets rang
with heavy traffic
in a kingdom of water

the next morning
every major periodical
reported on the Partido
Revolucionario Institucional (PRI) and how
like a fiesta
were the winds of lust
and diligence, and maybe
the election had been rigged,
but who wants to count?
in Chapultepec Park
the grasshoppers hopped
down quiet moonlit pathways

1967

in the Theosophical living room
we read from a book by
Madame Helene Blavatsky,
she wore gloves,
we ate in the kitchen
from a blue bowl
and listened to the radio,
it could be worse than love

I loved your jade eyes
and your thin strong body, your manner
of laughing, how you spoke my poems aloud

> *who was he and what did he accomplish, his*
> *apple red cheeks, his sculpted lips inviting me*
> *in the new century, pull him from the ether, you*
> *must translate the lost feeling, the ease of your love*
> *back then and the impossible well the news is*

how do the words fit into your heart?
when do we walk upstairs hand in hand
as if we had skimmed and
gone deeper? every letter
on my tongue I handed to you
that early evening, then reached
for your long blond hair, kissed your cheeks
and began slowly to unbutton
your shirt, we heard the robins outside
in the South Pasadena
night, the crowds would be
leaving the race track and the robins
would trill until they were worn out

I brought you upstairs, the odors
of the old house
were perfect, no one
would be home,

they'd gone
for several days, even the mole
who rented a room off the kitchen
had left, I felt
liberated and clear, it was '67, our war
worked its alchemical way
into the crevices of the republic

I thought
we would read poems forever, and
come to find meaning
behind every window, that
our understanding had grown deeper
than the passage of time, I saw only how
young we were, you were
a year out of high school, and I
was a student at Cal State

we visited my old poet friend in Hollywood,
he might have guessed at our love, I think
he imagined it, two decades later he whispered
"I knew. . ." but this was then
and we were thinking how love
could not end

parading into the commune
where you lived, your mother and father
twin spires of salt, gave us
a room of our own
until we floated off that hillside
across the San Fernando Valley

many nights, it did seem
like forever as the war tugged at us
and the music grew louder, I heard
the voice of Constantine Cavafy
and held your body close to mine
and lay quietly against your
smooth skin

later, when I came for you
and found the place abandoned
I panicked and drove up the coast
to where you had all
lived before, but they had
only rumors for me, I headed
further north, taking
side roads, finding
enough information
to keep going, asking how could he
leave me? driving and thinking
of the birds
and their chords, loud and
finally silent, our hands entwined

his parents must have
done this to separate us, something
he said to them, or they just had to
move on

or the year had died
and I hadn't noticed, alone
driving north, never going
back, driving
in a redwood grove, the
heavy shadows
falling over memory, driving
into the rain, I saw
my face in the glass
of the window, the wipers
moving at a fast clip, darkness
deepening I can only
cherish the idea that you were
looking, or maybe just thinking,
of me

Distance is Nearer

floating over
the smell of
asphalt and
the promise

fleeing from
light as it wiggles
across the field,
hoping

what can it
mean? the
towns seem
so far away

they stretch,
the feeling is of
hopelessness, of
living alone

the truth grates
on the edges
of light, no one
knows where

who believes
anything? the red
dawn is gray,
the gas pump drips

no one comes
along, true minds
hide in the brush
on the edges

a lizard darts
toward a viaduct,
metaphysics meets
gracious night

it is so distant
and so unfair,
nobody believes,
no one knows

the distance
is nearer by the
moment, who will
go there?

I ride a wave of
air, I touch the
quanta in the stream
of light, I believe

The Knowing Without Name

they know, they know
dogs, cats, alligators, centipedes
gnats, armadillos and zebras
they know, I can feel that they know
about moon tides, false hope
water and mud, zinc oxide and elemental
love, the gods know very well
that they have never died, they live
in the eyes, in the dog and cat and alligator
and centipede and gnat
and armadillo and zebra eyes,
the gods are in everything,
they smile in the knowledge
that doesn't cease, the
bitter knowing and the glorious
knowing and the knowing
without name

Visiting the Elder

he lies in bed but springs up
an old acrobat, five feet four inches tall
like Picasso and Stravinsky
bald with baseball cap as cover
no more wigs, ("they cost thousands")
bald as an eagle, bald but busy

old yet able to jump from bed
in a shared room so clean
no urine soaked sheets
no soiled utensils, halls are spic and span
a new universe of the fragile old
here the smell is young
like on the streets of the city

he gets up and beams
the beam and those big eyes of wonder
even in the old days when he'd complain
even when he thought
they were robbing him blind
and slighting him
not recognizing his fame

he thinks of greeting us
he points to trees outside
a beautiful sight brightening his simple room
he pays no attention to the flat screen TV
in the TV room, I try to interest him
in a stroll down the hallway
he diverts my attention
the outside world is strange and foreboding

an old man with a walker shuffles past
"that son of a bitch keeps going
to the end of the hall,
doesn't he realize there is nothing there?"

he sees out of ninety sets of eyes
he doesn't socialize

the attendant in the green smock
is invading his house
he wants me to lock the door
the door will never lock
even if this is his home now

I ask him to recite a poem
he reads one from 1956
written in Barcelona
his voice is strong
he reads with authority
as he did in the old days
no glasses, good vision
he reads, the room tremble
clear, ordinary, wondrous lines
about the extraordinary desire
to win a prize and to have eternal love
and when he is done we applaud
the two of us who have come to visit

I tell the attendants he is a poet
a famous poet
they didn't even know
I tell them we will return
and when we do can he go out for a walk
maybe we'll take 90 steps toward oblivion
and coffee at the café
down on the corner across the street
when we say goodbye
the elder poet extends
a warm hand, a small hand, a massive hand
it has been good of us to visit

"and by the way you should meet my mother
she looks less than 40
and she's at least 120 years old
she has a crown of diamonds
she walks down the hallway
like a queen to visit me here in my room"

From the Cabin at Bixby Canyon

now I burrow here in a sleeping bag
thinking of the early shade that covers
the Bixby world, it is a splendor
to gather wood, to make a fire, sit
before crackling flames, meditating long
hours, boiling water, pouring in
ground coffee, drinking slowly, rich scalding
brew, so like nobody, so intertwined
with the woods, so lofty, woodsman now

alone in the meditation cabin
at Bixby Creek, quietly attuned to
a hummingbird and cold coastal spirit,
mind abloom, reading Rilke,
relieved to find a European poet
for a coastal California reading. . .
thoughts of angels hovering near, blazing,
beautiful leopards leaping, lean, native
birds trilling, Ferlinghetti's lamp ablaze,
his cabin filled with shadows. I am sad
for my happiness, the elegies
are grass-blown, wind carved, funny, somberly
set for the visionary night soon to come
crashing on my eyes, what terrible truths trek
around the shoulder-hill to heart strewn hillside,
oh Rainer Maria Rilke, your name
spills off my brain, I watch your poem dance
from the German to the English, I wish
your words were nailed to my spirit, so torn
am I in this California fog, so borne
by nearby waves, so good in fallen sun,
end the poem, bring the leopards,
listen to the redwood, hear rough oak, bring
the elder, say the unspoken name, go
dive in the sky, fight no ocean muse, sit
facing the double door, this is your time,
sit here in meditation, but where
is the telephone? call your German friend
by his true name, offer a redwood name,

pry open the door, slam the window shut, laugh,
run to the end of the elegy, so lean
are these words, unmistakable and clear
the calling, yearning, desire, oh love
you are so me, so hopeless, you talk
only of yourself, you see only cool eyes
in the mirror of the stream

The Rage

tell rage
to stay outdoors
at least for one night,
take the anger
you fear and
fling it across the room
until it bounces,
call your sorrow
what it is,
name the sweeter sorrow
we call joy
and let it flood
the narrow channels
of your living dream,
put your envy
in a box
and close the lid,
open it
late at night
when you fear the eye
of the cosmos

what's on tap
says my neighbor?
is he kidding?
nothing, I mutter
under my breath,
except the rising
tides, the sick
ozone, the melting
ice, the cancerous
trees, the murder
of Babylon, the end
of America, the beginning
of an epic
with no good end

I take my rage by the throat
and embrace it
on the couch
in the front room
under a yellow lamp,
next to a wall
of books,
feeling helpless, yet
not entirely without hope
for a resolution made
out of a dot symbolizing
one of everything,
no more, no less

On the Drive South, I was Thinking

finally I see it, I mean the bleached
fronds of palm trees and the remains
of my mother, I see the shawls of women
who have gone, so what?
do these things matter
as the lights go down
and the newspaper comes banging
at the door? do you care
about the mountain range
and its broad elevations?
the winter snowfall will be
reported, trucks
will struggle up the grade,
coffee grounds will be thrown
into green garbage bins, and I will stop
to rest, turn the motor off
and listen
to cars speeding into the tunnel,
does it matter
who goes by? I can count
on none of them, they do not love
the great southern city
as I do, not its wide boulevards or
secretive alleys

I am deep
into the music, the window is
half way down, three hours more
and the outlands will wrap
around me, trailer parks
and suburban tracts, a shopping mall,
a pet cemetery, young men
on skateboards, the girls
on their cell phones, anger
in the silence, lots filled with weeds,
nobody knows, the genius
is in how the sewage holds, what the rabbit
can seize in the last free hills

all of this falls away
as I race
inside, is this how it was
in the caves? did the animal painters
give a damn about wisdom? I suspect
mindfulness was a constant, like
Autumn and its leaves and that
the bones of my family
will disappear here, right here
where I am sitting, I watch a trucker
leap into his cab, I see a man take a leak
against a tree, he won't walk fifty feet
to the public bathroom, here there are
liaisons, I might be able to meet
a hard bodied diamond merchant
with red eyes and a serpentine tongue
and find forgiveness in his arms, redemption
for the taking, but it is only
a dream passing in my thoughts, I am
going to the sprawl, my heart
is beating rapidly, just over the Grapevine
and along the barriers of night

Making Love to a Man

he is thinking of cold green agates
lying near the waves on an anonymous beach,
the sand burns, every muscle of the sun bleeds,
the cup in my palm trembles, I spill
water over the beachhead and feel salt air
rushing into my pores,
the starfish spread their tips toward implacable
space, we live here, we are the headlands
of seabirds and savage winds

he watches, I press lips to his thighs
and lick smooth skin,
then crawl across a subterranean chamber
to run my tongue up and down his belly
and go toward the shaft
to feel veins and go to where
I rest, help me keep to
the agate in my hand
I know the pain of another man,
remembering he was once a child as
I was a child, he will age
as I must, he will stop
in the middle of the night to rest an arm
on my shoulder, his blond mind
meets me on the narrow ridge

we walk to the precipice, I am released
into his release, we shower before dawn,
then turn oblivious, our clean sorrow
invites the sun

Snow Mountain

he took his hands
off the steering wheel and let the truck
guide itself in the ruts hammered
in the road from the ski lift
to Clancy's Bar

I loved the guys who drank
with their big hands and
broken hearts, bourbon
whiskey, cognac, Tobacco Man and
Big Clark, heir to a tool fortune
and the deputies in red winter coats

we hike to the summit
alone, or with *one hundred thousand songs*,
you observe a man of science studying
the water content of the snow
he will fill the rivers and flood
the low lands, on top of Snow Mountain
our madman sits holding
a rose shaped of ice

we are borne by pine trees, we learn
the path, the monks are
made of ice, they chew on it, they
split wood and burn it, screw the storm,
you endure, learn patience
solid as the desolate ridges

I loved that prefab hut purchased
from the military, the bend of its
wood frames, and the man
who was dying from a slow
disease off in a corner,
he loved to sit by a portal
and count snowflakes
as they fell on his wound

the snow dogs bark, halls are dusted in
frost, every flake is there, nothing melts
monks sing in unison
woodpecker
on a morning bough

the lift failed in that last
year, too much anger or not
enough, the bears scratched
at the horizon, you could feel
the sorrow, touch the
inevitability of loss

he sold the land and
moved out, the mountain
remains, deep snow
blinds me in sleep,
how I fall, I
rise, he is most likely gone

I place the mountain between my lips
in order to follow what is buried in air

we are swayed, devoured by
a dragon, he opens the door,
the snow is deep and hard
the edge is crisp
we stand together
before a cover of stars

The Women of Ciudad Juarez

she draws a sun dog out of the sky
followed by a jaguar,
tell me how far away
are the dreams, how near at hand
trucks wheezing across the land
carrying oil from rich fields
and tell me
about the women, but talk with a tremor
on gray sidewalks,
and pay homage to the labor
of those who love the rain

I come to you out of a crowd,
ancient lady, so far
away, yet so close by, I touch
your lips while a scorching noon
leaves us dizzy, tell me, always, how
did they bring you down? what words
fell from their mouths?

talk to the men who run the sugar processing
plants, the ones who own condominiums in high
mountain places faraway and how near
are the rabid corners, how near women
alone in the streetlights, alive on the dark-star,
alone in the house of lamps, speak into the microphone
and be quick, soothe the men
with your words, drink their mescal, eat their food

and let them argue about the ups and downs
of democracy, leave them to their stipends, give them
room to think, save the women for the dream
that tightens just before the distances glow and
grow near, talk to him, whisper in his ear, where is
Rosa now? who took Maria now? when will
the pottery lady return?

Carla, this is my new one, I wrote it this
morning so you might hear my words

43

in your mountain city surrounded by
condors, so I might whisper
the words, and be not quite appropriate,
the wistful dreams of those women who are
gone, the lost balladeer and those
who walked to the abyss on their own,
surrounded by stars

what assassins appear in the name
of the dog, the cat? "justice for the
murdered women" is nailed to the post
at the end of a road leading
to the unforgiven, how many
must disappear? what is a border?

whose shade crosses the drawn blinds
of the town? I imagine a street of shopkeepers
opening their stalls, we sell Indian blankets
and the choked up emotions of a republic
pecked by the beak of the eagle, and come
out of your torment, find the perpetrators
who raise their hands against your daughters, your
mothers, your sisters, your shadows, the bodies
wrapped in your bodies

give me a laurel wreath to place
on the steps of the library, I came here
and gave them a song, really, I am gone now, I
am dressed in a blouse and I wear beads
and have applied lipstick and rouge,
I am not of you, they come
to kill you, they are so far away and so
near at hand, they hide in their colonias,
they hire guards for the children,
they step over your broken bones,
what do they sing? they sing
of the sierras and
the dry arroyos

The Man at Eighty-Eight

he has gone to the Fortress of the Raven
where the sky and the river books
open their pages, and he has seen
the eyes of a cold mountain
against the blue madness
pigmented by the gods, and he has rented
five rooms in the Mission District
all these years, and not a penny more
to the albatross, nothing for the skylark
unless it's an entire life given to the muse

and he has seen the candle melt down
and the goddess smear lipstick
on the redwood tree, the ghost of Poe
with the ghost of Whitman and the ghost of Dickinson
and the fine hands of Shelley
the host of bastard angels
come swooping onto the screen

and he has taken the archaic words and bent them
for the post-mortem world and he has fallen
onto the wheels of time and will be carried away
with the roses and he will sing
to them and he will pay the landlord and slam the door
in the face of those sons of bitches
who murder the poets and throw them into the pits

and he will go home to his father
who never grew old and he will dance in Harlem
with the king and he will walk
across the wasteland and he will go shopping at "The Rainbow"
for golden rice and whole grain bread and he will
marvel at the stock boys and
he will think of many things to dance to
until the poem flies off his fingers like the raven
soaring toward doom

He Pushes Toward Abstraction

his push toward abstraction
drips out of the exhibition catalog
and sinks into the mind of later decades
his cranium filled with rage
the eyes grow weak, the hand, no longer steady
drops a brush onto the floor
his lily pads are mythological islands
he picks up a leaf from the path and examines
every line, the universe is deaf
the enemy is near, he cannot breathe
talk to the examiners, open the door to his studio
where there is a whisper of failure
the artist struggles to break his own heart
he becomes the trees, he cannot breathe

North Coast Poem

he comes running and then he sleeps in the rain,
he goes out to feel the breeze
through the apple trees and he comes running,
he goes out to find the country late at night
and feels the rain on his shoulders,
he goes out to find the trees and hears the deer
who are like light, so quickly they run
when he comes toward them,
squirrels jump onto the train of shadows,
badgers scamper through a hole in the fence,
raccoons pass an open door,
possums find a path
no one knows the wolverine
down by the woods

Sacramento River

his eye
is the only thing
I see,
the ship will
rest in his eye,
the bridge may
close, leaving us
in the flat flood plain
long enough
to find the banks, we
define this
as a river, here is
a route
of weeds, of water, of
delta, a way of body
and mind, the river,
the river, you don't even know
if it is there,
we only have
this time to say hello,
are you charting the
water? do you have
maps?
may I ask the lecturer a question
before the snow melts
and moves along,
is there such a place as
paradise? we are convinced
the conversation
comes to an end,
I yield to the rhythm

Turning to See You

turning to see you
asleep, your
graying hair, my charcoal brain filled
with an image of the wild

your body forms a question mark
I touch a strand of hair falling
over your forehead

the animals
in your body
are poised to
cross the river

I turn the other way and
cover my head in
the comforter, it is time
to face the rapids, time now
to find a name

At Land's End

we must know what the lupine brings
early in the century, or how to form words
from silence within the emptiness
where land and desire end

the power emerges, a pelican dives
for his prey, on the horizon
the gods assemble, we find light
on the bones of love

where no voice rises
the signs go askew
anger beyond hope emerges, blind men
seize power through deceit

so goes the bread, lone seal lounging
belly to the sun, a sun-prophet, present, ageless
waiting for the tide, the hot sand a home
within the vast house of being

alone

At the Mouth of the River

I listen only to the sailors
now and to the fear they feel
when the dream takes
an unfortunate turn
the cloud lingers
and love is cast
like a net over the mouth
of the river, dangerous sand bars
keep the pilot boats running,
the Coast Guard patrols
regularly, I am inside of these things
busily at work, I wake in the night
as people dream

you must listen when I am talking to you
said the old man in the water
he holds an oil lamp to
my eyes, the pilot takes out the map
of his mind and unfolds it, love
is a river in your mouth, your tongue
touches mine, the indigenous people
living here fished these banks, they went out
in reed boats to test the limits
imposed by need, now you hear
me, said the old man, I am a ghost
in your dream, walking, awake as
any man, he pushes the barge
over the sand bar, he lifts the fear
I have of ending up alone, how do
you manage? where do you go
when the cloud is snagged
on a tree at the Point?
I see you now, I hide in the image
you have of me, I touch your beard
and fall to the river
I am carried along, soon the gorge
will rise, the pilot boat
will never rest
they will wait for the call

on the open sea, some of the sailors
think of the water

at the mouth of the river
I stand on the bank and wait
I hold a cup of coffee
this is the beginning, now you need to
pay attention, you are running
within, you affirm
my love, I must try to hold you
where the water threatens

The Old Song Remains

these arrogant young men
are in love, we follow their steps
down the corridor
past the naval academy where
you may go for cold lemonade, you drop
your anchor
in the heart
of the song, do you mean
infatuation? shades of luck
and no luck at all, in love
with, who knows
the power better than those
who remain lost in language? she hid
in her dining room, we
listened as she told her triumphs, yet
even with them she is sad, frustrated, the paintings
behind her she cannot
begin to recognize, I have a fondness for
her vanity, I love how
the water
forces its way out of the core, how the ferns
congregate
the poor are hidden,
the infirm are paraded only
in dreams, we step
into the furnace, here's the falcon
on a wire, here's
the cold art
we think of
as we bend
toward the truth, did you say "bent?" we are
seemingly
like a bow, the old song
remains
heroic, we twist
and turn, we speak for the land, they are
putting
stones into our mouths the young men
so arrogant

are they not?
your mystery is
if you feel your wave, the falcons
own the
sky, here are azure
bricks
he throws
out the last
angel
with his archaic hard-on and his
deer mask, he is holding
a lot of soil, is he not
a bit
taken aback by the music of those who think
they are in love? what do you feel
when you are
in love?
I see the ghost
of the harbor
after the bars and cafes have shut their doors, the chairs
have been folded and stacked, lights bob
up and down
on one of the yachts, we step
across
the memory, you are trapped
on a branch
from the past, you fall
face forward
on the sidewalk, you may see your broken teeth
in the mirror, there are trees
in the mirror, we find the cosmos there, we
were charioteers, we hide behind the black rose, we
were
on a pilgrimage, we are
the ill-fated crew, we defend the fortress
at the end of the story, we confront the lion before
the gate, we walk
among the olive trees

in the late afternoon, he keeps
her hidden behind
the bushes until the rains
wash the grime
away and she is radiant, he says
my mother came for two hours, she has been gone
one quarter of a century, yet out of kindness
she stepped into the room, we were not yet fully awake
he needs to be cared
by the state, we are
re-reading the poems of Rimbaud
while walking the dog
near Fort Funston, there is garbage all along the beach,
you find needles
mixed with seaweed, the dog barks
at the sky, I think when I die
they will
seize my heart, they will sew it up and
forgive me, now he is
closing the double gate. he in advanced old age, I listen
but cannot make sense
of his words, he tells me
to come over, don't come over, he
dresses like a woman
and walks by the harbor
as they bring in
a barge filled with
statues
of the Furies, and we
are simply sitting under an awning
waiting for
a word of warning, the story
is about love, does he
make sense
of the land on which he has chosen
to settle?

The Length

it is the "cruel" of the
ocean, not what you see, the cruel
solitude, the inevitable
loss, it is the land in your
reverie, the length of it, the loss
you taste, the feel of the
words as they form
in what is called the heart

Guadalupe

what force destroys
us? why? I fear pain
when it creeps up

the hill, I push petals
away from eyelids of flowers
and find a beast
through a taxicab window, a coyote

with heavy paws, a dog snarling
a cat leaping, a crow dead
a snake turning green
in a brown forest, a roaring

fire, Guadalupe in a flood of leaves
when summer began, I find
you groping in the darkness
hold me, leave me, laugh

curse, ring me up
on every available line

Meditation Nearing Sixty

sixty years in July, It's a bit embarrassing
I was never meant to be old
like this, just like I wasn't meant to serve in the military, or
to sit on a jury, or to
fend for myself as other men do, the sun is climbing
in my window, it is burning a hole in my solitude, it is asking me
onto the deck and into the garden, here in the garden
I can play with my dog or read from Lorca, or
simply stare at the bushes
and the trees, I have watered my plants through two desert wars
and taken the measure of the misery
we've caused, the pain and suffering
we, ourselves, come in with and go out with,
I find the shadow of the blackbird warring with the bluebird and
when I listen to Beethoven, or "Bitches Brew" by Miles Davis
something like hope rises
out of the doom and I think
it is good to make music, it is good to write poems, it is fine
to make paintings and to sit alone
for the afternoon
in meditation:
sixty winters, sixty dreams, one day
of reckoning, one father, one mother, one sister, one lover, one
dog, a garden, a redwood deck, a work room, a bedroom,
a guest room, a living room, a dining room, a kitchen, a TV room
all the ordinary stuff of the middle class...
a new born child clutching
a dream of the one poem
that rises from our common desire

Being In Love

he was quiet and self-assured, the wine
sat on the table
in that joyous light associated
with angry historical angels
no longer recognizable, he had been a research librarian
at UC Berkeley in the time of such luminaries
as Baudelaire and Wordsworth, he was eclectic, capable of
stripping the bark from Homer, fully aware
of language and its lack of power to comprehend
the unrecognizable power of love
because he also knew
what we call love is just another string
in the unlimited order
of nothing, he poured us each
a glass, the women watched
the ferry, a bell rang for the man being brought home
from the medical center
lying in a coffin, they had put
straw in the cavities
where his eyes had once been
there were whispers of love and lust
in the olive grove, we were allowed to walk there
when the pharmacist opened the gate
to what he called paradise, it's just a hidden grove
almost timeless, the bleached green leaves
were brittle to the touch, I was
charmed by their fragility, I wanted to say
how much I love to think of trees
I thought of what extraordinary love
(for example) Monet had given to the
poplars, or was it they who gave to Monet?
and everything talks to everything else, even
the silent man talks to Socrates, even
the painter forgives his mountain, I guess
we left the grove
thinking there were seabirds at the gate and
the donkeys were braying as the rich German
publisher led his wives and x-wives, along with
servants and retainers, to the mansion

high above the house where the famous artist
spends a few weeks each year
I would like to examine
the eyes again, the pronouns
of Walt Whitman, how do you run
as fast as the ridiculous things
poets say about love?
we have changed nothing, not a damn
thing, not one centimeter, not a dime's worth
as he locked the gate
to the grove, we said we need time
to let go of love, we need a treatise
on the improbability of knowing
why this feeling is here, this luminous
loss, these empty eyes, these rocks
we place where the hunger had been, this gold mask
we hammer into shape, this tree at the end
of land, swell of the nearby waves beyond
the harbor, the loss of the woman who had stood
alone, the yachts from distant islands, the elders
on their blue benches, the German magazine publisher
comes to the port for scotch and soda
at the red benches, there is a bodyguard and
a secretary, beyond love
we claim emptiness as a monument
a vision is given to the librarian, a gift
in words we cannot wholly decipher, the hawks
fly over the coast, a sense of being
here in time, of knowing it is impossible
to trim love to a few words, or
to a tree, or to a wave

From the Canyon Outward

I scratch my head in the late afternoon
as the sun drops onto the canyon floor
a ball of fire to be bounced
like a child's toy across seven levels
of the mind, the flames will dwindle
the mosquitoes will return
donned in insect armor, warriors of the air
followed by a single hummingbird
remembered in the books of nowhere

my dog has nothing to say
the telephone meditates on the table
by the kitchen, it will not ring
the polar bears leap onto fragile ice
they drown in blue water
the sun howls, a wintry owl
turns upside down, nobody knows
where we come from, maybe
from a house in the woods

when I fall into the silence
of my bed
I think of graying shadows
and the end of summer, I hold
imaginary leaves against
my chest and move a hand
to where the shade falls between
twin shafts of the moon
that have found their way
into the room, I think the owl
is hooting, winter and summer
loosen their grip

when I melt
it is because of voices
from the most unusual places
I am alone, alive, in love, above
the fray, capable of listening
to the music of signs

and symbols that have
a common ancestry

from the canyon
to entanglement
of metaphor, from a quest for affirmation
to beautiful nonsense, a door
to the open field
a path up the side of the mountain
and down again, a place
to sit in a café, a corner of the local bar
the roar of a bear in my head

I don't get drunk anymore
I sit and think
of demonic angels
and angelic demons, artists and
art dealers, leaders and the led
I hold an empty cup
going to the garden
half buried by our deck, it is difficult
to believe in anything but
what is given, quietly, to me

Reading Facing East

it is not possible to hold
your shadow in my arms, or to place my palm
face down on your side of the bed, I reach
for the word, I am reading, facing east
the late poems of a trickster, he dresses
like bamboo and
talks to a phantom woman
who leaves her song under the eaves of his
house, now I lean
on the terrace before the remains of the last
light, the waves
below "trouble deft heaven"

our red flowers have taken
the steam out of the yellow ones, I try
to water them everyday, I give the bamboo
their portion, a hummingbird
waited
until I had finished
and arched
over the pots

over the secret
of flowers and veins
of bamboo

Carla

Carla, if I were 23
and a poet from Ecuador, a young man
named Amor or Soledad and my hair
had not turned gray and my hips
did not hurt climbing the hills
here in San Francisco

and you were 63 and you
were from here and I was
as indigenous as pumice
in your native land
and you kept thinking
he is so young, he is so handsome

Carla you are overflowing
with 23 years, I try to push them
into place, you are skipping and jumping
as I muse
while I huddle
in my room, alone, you are
singing and the piano
is dropping its keys on the floor
and I am scrambling for words

if I were 23
and from Ecuador, here
with my poems and if I found you
sitting at an outdoor table
of a neighborhood cafe
would you read my words of Spanish
and trim the ash
from my raven hair
and find the song
of what it means
to bring our bodies and our dreams
along?

High Sierra

a lizard wiggles from
the shadow of
a boulder and slices the air
with its tail

canyons of sunlight
cover cold noon
and trickle along
precipitous ridges

a man emerges
from a lichen-
lined cave, his
cougar smiles

the eagle guards
our back,
twin hikers
follow a switchback
and head
for lean pine trees,
clearly we are driven
to see and to accept

and to believe this
inheritance: deer, bear,
badger, coon,
wolverine, jay,
name a spirit
for the body
as it sinks

if only my song
could know
the whole terrain,
a busted god
lives in the
jagged wild

how old are
the clouds? what do
you say to the
branches
of rock, or to the light
haze of snow
on the brow
of a giant?

cling to a spike
of ice, a tremor
in the trail, dusk
on a ring of
grass, dew
on a half-burnt log

the body is
a mountain
of conifer and
roots, tendrils
glow in the rich
core, a dancer
drops out of the
mid-morning sun, at noon
all is a furnace

in the late afternoon
we imagine mortality and
bend to pick a
rusty blade of grass
from the handsome land
right by the creek and
hold it like a wand

To an Old Friend

yes, I was wronged
by your barbs
and quick judgments,
I was thrown against white stucco
coming
and going back home,
watching an elder
grow older,
haunting our
haunts, remembering
Crazy Jack
who bled ink, his girl friend
Mary who sang with us
on a bench
in the cemetery
until the guard chased us
past the tomb
of Tyrone Power, you
may guess
I press the concrete mesh
to my lips
and remain here
on top of your head

you may dance a jig
in an orchestra
and talk to me
out of the mud
and muck
of an alley or
rise like vapor
in my room,
I'd say you were right
about the dead
who march and the living
who cannot love

do you remember that
Plymouth with the

loud horn? how we drove
along the boulevards
haunted and
humorous? we needed
a stage and
a director to tell us
how to unwrap those expensive
cigars we took
to the fights, we'd shout and
boo, laugh,
curse the referees and joke
as fat people
wedged into
their seats

you liked it
when we had those
three day drunks
against the miracle
of light and
spoke disdain
for almost
everything that moved,
I'd drive home
to my room off
La Brea, thoughtful
and silent and would
sit for hours
on the red couch
with uneven springs

you met the cowgirl
from Utah
and Liza, wise
in drug land
and now in
a home, what a mad
mix, you dug
the city up, tossed it

across the flowing
traffic
and leaned-in
as we drove toward
the beach with six
packs in the backseat

I will travel
down and then
back again, down to
the stucco and
geranium beds, over
to the smiling
corpse and home
again, my thoughts
settle on solitude
and the great remains
as the engines
turn and the
turbines
burn, it is
a long
ride in either case,
and is
my pleasure

Big Sur...

where
the coast is wildly at peace
and far beyond time

the trees and shrubs
are profuse, a creek runs there
and meets the ocean

the body finds its way
to the mind, when the body
goes, so goes the coast

so goes the canyon, yet
the gulls still fly, the language
of salt and sand and tidal pond

still twine, I hold every question
like a candle and hike
deep down the path

in my mind, here the grass
rustles in the breeze, all
possibilities drift

and we are free

by Dennis Letbetter

Neeli Cherkovski is a longtime contributor to the West Coast literary scene. Emerging from the Los Angeles underground of the Sixties, Cherkovski is an applauded poet, critic and literary biographer. He has written ten books of poetry, including the award winning *Leaning Against Time*, *Elegy for Bob Kaufman* and *Animal*; two acclaimed biographies, *Bukowski: A Life* and *Ferlinghetti: A Biography*; his book, *Whitman's Wild Children* (a collection of critical memoirs), has become an underground classic. In the late 1960s Cherkovski co-edited the poetry anthology *Laugh Literary and Man the Humping Gun*s with Charles Bukowski. Since 1975, Neeli has lived and worked in San Francisco. For ten years he was Writer-in-Residence at New College of California, where he taught literature and philosophy.